Redford Township District Library
25320 West Six Mile Road
Redford, MI 48240

www.redford.lib.mi.us

Hours:

Mon-Thur 10-8:30
Fri-Sat 10-5
Sunday (School Year) 12-5

D1542351

JUN 19 2000

Popular Cat Library

American Shorthair Cat

Karen Commings

Published in association with T.F.H. Publications, Inc.,
the world's largest and most respected publisher of pet literature

Chelsea House Publishers
Philadelphia

CONTENTS

Popular Cat Library

Abyssinian Cat
American Shorthair Cat
Bengal Cat
Birman Cat
Burmese Cat
Exotic Shorthair Cat
Himalayan Cat
Maine Coon Cat
Persian Cat
Ragdoll Cat
Scottish Fold Cat
Siamese Cat

This edition © TFH Publications, Inc., 1 TFH Plaza, Neptune City, NJ 07753. This special library bound edition is made expressly for Chelsea House Publishers, a division of Main Line Book Company.

Library of Congress Cataloging-in-Publication Data

Commings, Karen.
Guide to owning an American shorthair / by Karen Commings.
p.   cm. — (Popular cat library)
Summary: A guide to the history, feeding, grooming, exhibition, temperament, health, and breeding of American shorthair cats.
ISBN 0-7910-5458-6 (hc.)
1. American shorthair cat Juvenile literature.   {1. American shorthair cat.   2. Cats.
3. Pets.]   I.Title. II. Series.
SF449.A45C86 1999
636.8'22—dc21   99-36715
                                                                          CIP

The Guide to Owning an
American
Shorthair Cat

Karen Commings

CONTENTS

Photography: Deborah Carney, Chanan, Karen Commings, Chris Fogg, Isabelle Francais.

3 9082 07754 0444

RE 413

© T.F.H. Publications, Inc.

Distributed in the UNITED STATES to the Pet Trade by T.F.H. Publications, Inc., 1 TFH Plaza, Neptune City, NJ 07753; on the Internet at www.tfh.com; in CANADA by Rolf C. Hagen Inc., 3225 Sartelon St., Montreal, Quebec H4R 1E8; Pet Trade by H & L Pet Supplies Inc., 27 Kingston Crescent, Kitchener, Ontario N2B 2T6; in ENGLAND by T.F.H. Publications, PO Box 74, Havant PO9 5TT; in AUSTRALIA AND THE SOUTH PACIFIC by T.F.H. (Australia), Pty. Ltd., Box 149, Brookvale 2100 N.S.W., Australia; in NEW ZEALAND by Brooklands Aquarium Ltd., 5 McGiven Drive, New Plymouth, RD1 New Zealand; in SOUTH AFRICA by Rolf C. Hagen S.A. (PTY.) LTD., P.O. Box 201199, Durban North 4016, South Africa; in JAPAN by T.F.H. Publications, Japan—Jiro Tsuda, 10-12-3 Ohjidai, Sakura, Chiba 285, Japan. Published by T.F.H. Publications, Inc. MANUFACTURED IN THE UNITED STATES OF AMERICA BY T.F.H. PUBLICATIONS, INC.

HISTORY OF THE AMERICAN SHORTHAIR

The American Shorthair cat boasts a legacy as expansive as the history of the United States. The first short-haired cats were reputed to have crossed the Atlantic Ocean with the Pilgrims on the Mayflower when they came to America in 1620. Valued as a mouser, the sturdy, athletic cat that was the precursor to today's pedigreed American Shorthair was expected to earn her keep onboard by preventing the ship's food supplies from being devoured by rats and mice. Once cats landed at Plymouth Rock, they had to continue to work for a living if they wanted to retain the comfort of home life with the early settlers. Those cats desiring a more independent way of life in the new land were free to explore, scavenging for food and propagating their species.

Along with the early pioneers, short-haired cats ventured inland and across the continent, populating the New World with members of their own kind. The human-feline partnership continued to be one of mutual benefit. Wherever humans had food and grain stores that needed protection from the New World's

Reputed to have come to America with the Pilgrims on the Mayflower, the American Shorthair evolved over the centuries into a sturdy, muscular breed.

The pedigreed American Shorthair that competes in today's show ring is the result of more than 100 years of controlled and selective breeding.

rodent population, cats congregated to perform the task. Over the centuries that followed, the sturdy, muscular, working feline established herself as the native American cat.

FROM HUMBLE BEGINNINGS

Although the American Shorthair shares its heritage with the cats that freely roamed the streets, fields, and barnyards of America for more than 200 years, the pedigreed American Shorthair that competes in today's show ring is the result of more than 100 years of controlled and selective breeding. Your pet cat may resemble the purebred

Today the American Shorthair is consistently one of the ten most popular breeds of cats according to the Cat Fanciers' Association.

American Shorthair, a fact that is testimony to a common ancestry, but the pedigreed lines of this handsome, sweet-faced feline owe their existence to both human intervention and the good graces of Mother Nature.

Until the start of the 20th century, the domestic short-haired cat attracted little attention from cat fanciers. The favorite native breed of the American show ring at that time was a long-haired beauty known as the Maine Coon. Ironically, the first registered short-haired cat in the United States was a male orange tabby that had been imported in 1901 from Great Britain. The cat, named Belle of Bradford, was registered as simply a "shorthair."

Around the same time that Belle was gaining fame, cat fanciers became more interested in the sleeker or more unusual foreign breeds of cats that were being introduced into the US, such as the slender Siamese and long-haired beauties such as Persians and Turkish Angoras. Some of these imported felines escaped the confines of their homes or were allowed to run loose by careless owners. Whether the exotic foreign cats met their newfound freedom with enthusiasm or disdain, cats being cats, they commingled with the native felines—whether purebred or not—creating kittens with varieties of coat lengths, body types, and colors. Cat fanciers, wishing to preserve the natural beauty of those cats native to America, acquired excellent specimens and began selectively breeding them to perfect their color and coat patterns.

Once American short-haired cats were incorporated into the Shorthair breed, the official designation was changed to Domestic Shorthair, a name that continued until 1966. At that point, the Cat Fanciers' Association (CFA) changed the name to American Shorthair to differentiate it from the plentiful, randomly bred short-haired cats found in shelters across the country or roaming alone or in feral packs on US streets. The proof of a purebred American Shorthair is in the litter rather than the pudding. A purebred ASH, as they are affectionately called by breeders, will consistently produce kittens of uniform type.

At first, the cat registries established few requirements for registering Domestic Shorthairs, many of which were of unknown origin. They were often shown in household pet classes, and, if they were shown in championship classes amid the sophisticated Europeans, the working class Domestic Shorthairs were received with only a lukewarm reaction at best and unkindly at worst. An open registration policy proceeded intermittently, allowing breeders to register any short-haired cat as a Domestic Shorthair. As a result, breeders attempted to expand their gene pools by introducing randomly bred cats into their lines as well as other breeds to their lines to produce new colors and alter the type. This practice, called outcrossing, is regulated by the association in which the breed is registered. The American Shorthair owes its more rounded head and substantial body in part to some Persian mixed in its bloodlines. The silver tabby, one of the most popular colors of American Shorthair, is a result of outcrossing with chinchilla Persians. It was also outcrossing with Persians that produced the Exotic Shorthair breed.

In addition to outcrossing with other breeds to improve the American Shorthair type, the American Shorthair has been outcrossed with other breeds to improve her color, strength, and appearance. Outcrossing the Siamese with an American Shorthair produced the Colorpoint Shorthair and outcrossing the Burmese with an American Shorthair resulted in the Bombay. American Shorthairs played a part in producing the Ocicat, the Snowshoe, and the Scottish Fold, and they are still allowable outcrosses for some breeds today.

A PLACE IN THE SUN
Although it was a long time coming, American Shorthairs finally attained a place of honor

These American Shorthair kittens are characteristically strong by tradition and have no genetic health problems. They may live 15 to 20 years.

within the cat fancy. The first American Shorthair Grand Champion in the CFA was a blue-eyed white female named NorMont's Angelique, born in 1948. Progress continued with the new breed, but it wasn't until 1950 that a stud book was printed tracing the lineage of the American Shorthair.

Today, the American Shorthair is consistently one of the ten most popular breeds of cats, according to the CFA. At the show hall and in the ring, the American Shorthair has won her share of awards and prizes, including CFA *Cat of the Year* and *Kitten of the Year,* and multiple Grand Champions, Grand Premiers, and regional winners.

American Shorthairs, with their coats of many colors, sweet expressions, and mild dispositions, make great pets. Because they are strong and have no genetic health problems, they can live upward of 15 to 20 years. If you decide to purchase this all-American animal and bring her into your home, prepare yourself for a long-term commitment and years of companionship and love.

To retain the comforts of home, the ancestors of the American Shorthair had to work hard as mousers in the barns and granaries of the early settlers.

AMERICAN SHORTHAIR CHARACTER

The beautiful, muscular American Shorthair is a low-maintenance, easygoing feline companion that will provide you with years of comfort and love. Because of their extensive heritage as working cats and mousers, American Shorthairs are self-reliant and possess good hunting instincts. Breeders and owners of American Shorthairs attest to their intelligence and problem-solving abilities. They can calculate solutions to problems and

Because American Shorthairs are playful and alert, they seem to establish a special bond with kids.

eliminate obstructions to things they want to do, such as finding a container of treats that you've hidden somewhere in the kitchen or opening that canister of cat food. Opening closet and cupboard doors is well within their grasp, and you may find yourself having to install latches on them to keep your American Shorthair from investigating places she shouldn't. Don't expect your ASH to have an aversion to water. An ancestry that encompassed life outdoors may make your cat inclined to want to drink from a faucet rather than a bowl and to play in running water. However, just because the American Shorthair might have spent time outside in her distant past, keep yours safely indoors to ensure her long life and well-being.

American Shorthairs are exuberant, energetic, and extremely alert. In spite of their natural curiosity, they are cautious and evaluate a situation before plunging into it. American Shorthairs like to observe everything that is going on while not missing a beat. The cats are generally calm, patient, laid back, and completely suitable for both quiet or moderately active households.

Training American Shorthairs is easy. They understand a lot of

Adult American Shorthairs are polite, but they enjoy "supervising" all home activities.

words, and, as a result, animal trainers use many American Shorthairs for commercials. They can be trained to stay away from valuable breakables and places that you decide they should not go, such as the dinner table or kitchen counters. You will find your American Shorthair learning lessons all by herself in addition to those you teach. You may find your ASH sitting by the window awaiting your return because she has learned the times of your arrival and departures and the sound of your car as it comes down the street.

American Shorthairs are affectionate and enjoy being with their people. Your ASH is likely to follow you around the house as you take care of daily chores, awaiting a time when the two of you can settle down and get comfortable. You might find your ASH lying on your chest or by your side as you watch TV. Most American Shorthairs, although bonding with one special person in the household, will share their devotion with all members of the family.

Breeders and owners attest to the American Shorthair's loving disposition. They make receptive, entertaining

companions that are always there for you to hold and talk to when you need a friend. While your ASH may not always want to sit on your lap, you may find her napping or snoozing close by.

Other words breeders use to describe the ASH are moderate, tolerant, patient, aware, and sweet. They are gentle and get along well with people of all ages, dogs, and other breeds of cats. They are moderate in build—

American Shorthairs can calculate solutions to problems and eliminate obstructions to things they want to do.

neither cobby like a Persian or sleek like a Siamese—and moderate in personality as well—neither couch potato nor curtain climber.

A CAT FOR FAMILIES

American Shorthairs are people-oriented and do well with children, provided the children are educated and supervised to make certain they treat the cats correctly. Because American Shorthairs are playful and alert, they seem to establish a special bond with kids. They love to be petted and spoiled by adults as well. You may find your ASH sleeping and playing with your children, and, when she loses patience with the children, simply leaving the room or seeking a high place to get away.

If your family includes other pets as well as youngsters, an American Shorthair will adapt well to living with them, even if the pets are Dobermans or Dalmatians. You even may find

Because American Shorthairs understand a lot of words, animal trainers are able to hire them out to star in television commercials.

that your ASH has the upper hand in the relationship.

KITTENS

ASH kittens are sweet, lovable, active, and alert. Having an ASH kitten in your household is like having a two- or three-year-old baby around. If you've brought two into your home, you will find that they love to play with each other (without being rascals) and are always on the go. You will find your ASH kitten running across your furniture and up her cat tree, but never up your drapes or screens. When the kittens tire, they sleep just as hard as they play. The ASH physically matures at around three to four years of age, so expect yours to retain her kitten playfulness for a long time.

ADULTS

Adult American Shorthairs are calm creatures that like to be with their people but not necessarily on their laps. In all things they are polite, willing to supervise all home activities, lie on the book or newspaper you're attempting to read, watch dinner being prepared, or simply stay by your side. They enjoy petting, combing, and occasional hugs, but may not like being picked up and carried around. The males are more relaxed and outgoing, more puppylike, while the females may be more sophisticated and aloof.

Adult American Shorthairs are moderately active, not lazy or complacent. They also are moderately demanding, and you may find your ASH waking you up in the morning by pawing your face to get you to either empty the litter box or make breakfast. Adult American Shorthairs are eager to please and cooperate with you and your plans, whether it is taking them to a cat show or to the veterinarian.

WHEN COMPANY COMES

Your American Shorthair will enjoy the attention of your guests as much as she will members of your family, and may run to the door when the doorbell rings to see who is coming. Even though your ASH is interested in company, you may find her

waiting to see what kind of person you've invited into your home before lavishing the guest with affection.

NOT A LOT TO SAY

American Shorthairs don't talk a lot, saving their vocal expressions to tell you when they want something, like dinner or a bedtime snack. When they do utter a few sounds, their voices have soft, gentle tones. They differ from the gutsy, raspy sound of a Siamese, a breed known as much

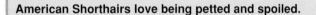
American Shorthairs love being petted and spoiled.

American Shorthairs don't "talk" much, saving their vocal expressions to tell you when they want something, like dinner or a bedtime snack.

for its voice as well as its looks. ASH cats may even put different sounds together, making what sound like cat sentences.

Your ASH will love to purr, the sound that is so consoling to cat owners, and will shower you with its humming on many occasions.

PLAYTIME

Your American Shorthair will always be ready for games with you and other pets in your household. Expect your American Shorthair to play, even as an adult. Feather toys, mice on strings, kitty fishing rods, ping pong balls, and crumpled paper balls are toys that you should have around the house for your ASH to play with. Because the ASH is a born hunter, you may find yours stalking her play prey in the form of a stuffed mouse or bird, then throwing it up in the air repeatedly and carrying it around in her mouth, meowing at the same time. Many enjoy a good game of hide-and-seek with their owners.

ASHs are athletic and agile, never klutzy or clumsy. They love to jump up high when playing, and we are always most surprised to see their strength when doing so. They love to race around and will entertain themselves when you are not available. In spite of her desire for fun, the ASH is not rowdy or destructive.

Words that breeders use to describe the American Shorthair are moderate, tolerant, patient, aware, and sweet. They are gentle and get along well with people of all ages, dogs, and other breeds of cats.

WOULD YOU MAKE A GOOD OWNER?

American Shorthairs live a long time and require as a caregiver someone who is dedicated to their care and well-being. An ASH will form a bond with her owner, so it's important for anyone buying one to make a real commitment and to be settled. No cat likes a loud, disorganized, unfriendly, or unloving household, so if you can provide a comfortable and calm environment, an American Shorthair will thrive in your home.

Because the ASH likes company, you must be willing to spend time with your cat and establish a bond of trust. The more love your ASH gets from you, the more she will give in return.

Several centuries of working as a mouser for her keep have resulted in a cat of strength, endurance, agility, and grace.

THE AMERICAN SHORTHAIR STANDARD AND COLORS

The American Shorthair is a muscularly built cat, and several centuries of working for her keep have resulted in an animal of strength, endurance, agility, and grace. To the untrained eye, most American Shorthairs will be adequate examples of the breed. If you have a pet-quality American Shorthair, it will provide you with the same love and companionship as a show-quality one, but if you are planning to compete in cat shows or to become a breeder, it is best to familiarize yourself with the standard for the breed and learn to recognize an outstanding specimen.

THE STANDARD

Anyone who has watched an Olympic gymnastics meet or skating competition knows that competitors have a standard of quality against which their performances are judged. Likewise, cats entering show competitions are evaluated against a breed standard that has been established by the association in which they are registered. Simply stated, breed standards are ideals of appearance against which each cat is judged. The winning cat in each category should most closely match the standard for its breed.

One of the most striking and recognizable American Shorthair cats is the silver tabby, with its dense black, classic tabby pattern on a sterling silver background.

Each cat registry applies a certain number of points to each of the various features, based on their relative importance. Judges, however, don't mentally add up the points for each cat in the show ring as they are judging. Rather, they look for features that don't conform to breed standard and that might disqualify a cat.

AMERICAN SHORTHAIR BREED STANDARD

The American Shorthair standards may vary slightly from registry to registry. Unlike the dog fancy, which is regulated exclusively by the American Kennel Club, the cat fancy has more than six US and Canadian registries that track the lineage or pedigree of the members' cats. The largest registry in the world is the Cat Fanciers' Association, and it is the CFA standard that is reproduced here with kind permission.

POINT SCORE

Head (including size and shape of eyes, ear shape, and set and structure of nose)—30

Body (including shape, size, bone, and length of tail)—30

Coat—15

Color (Tabby pattern = 10 points; Color =10 points)—20

Eye Color—5

GENERAL: The American Shorthair is a true breed of working cat. The conformation should be adapted for working with no part of the anatomy so exaggerated as to foster weakness. The general effect should be that of a strongly built, well balanced, symmetrical cat with conformation indicating power, endurance, and agility.

SIZE: Medium to large. No sacrifice of quality for sake of size. Females may be less massive in all respects than males and should be rewarded equally if overall balance is correct.

PROPORTIONS: Slightly longer than tall. (Height is profile measure from top of shoulder blades to ground. Length is profile measure from tip of breastbone to rear tip of buttocks.) Viewed from the side, body can be divided into three equal parts—from tip of breastbone to elbow, from elbow to front of hind leg, and from front of hind leg to rear tip of buttocks. Length of tail is equal to distance from shoulder blades to base of tail.

HEAD: Large, with full-cheeked face giving the impression of an oblong just slightly longer than wide. Sweet, open expression. Viewed from front, head can be divided in two equal parts; from base of ears to middle of eyes and from middle of eyes to chin tip.

EARS: Medium size, slightly rounded at tips and not unduly open at base. Distance between ears, measured from lower inner corners, twice the distance between eyes.

FOREHEAD: Viewed in profile, forehead forms smooth, moderately convex continuous curve flowing over top of head into neck. Viewed from front, there is no dome between ears.

EYES: Large and wide with upper lid shaped like half an almond (cut lengthwise) and lower lid shaped in a fully rounded curve. At least width of one eye between eyes. Outer corners set very slightly higher than inner corners. Bright, clear and alert.

NOSE: Medium length, same width for entire length. Viewed in profile, there is a gentle concavely curved rise from bridge of nose to forehead.

MUZZLE: Squared. Definite jowls in mature males.

JAWS: Strong and long enough to success– fully grasp prey. Both level and scissors bites considered equally correct. (In level bite, top and bottom front teeth meet evenly. In scissors bite, inside edge of top front teeth touches outside edge of lower front teeth.)

CHIN: Firm and well-developed, forming perpendicular line with upper lip.

NECK: Medium in length, muscular and strong.

BODY: Solidly built, powerful, and muscular with well-developed shoulders, chest, and hindquarters. Back broad, straight and level. Viewed in profile, slight slope down from hip bone to base of tail. Viewed from above, outer lines of body parallel.

LEGS: Medium in length and bone, heavily muscled. Viewed from rear, all four legs straight and parallel with paws facing forward.

PAWS: Firm, full and rounded, with heavy pads. Toes: five in front, four behind.

TAIL: Medium long, heavy at base, tapering to abrupt blunt end in appearance but with normal tapering final vertebrae.

COAT: Short, thick, even and hard in texture. Regional and seasonal variation in coat thickness allowed. Coat dense enough to protect from moisture, cold, and superficial skin injuries.

PENALIZE: Excessive cobbiness or ranginess. Very short tail.

DISQUALIFY: Cats showing

A pet-quality American Shorthair will provide you with the same love and companionship as a show-quality one.

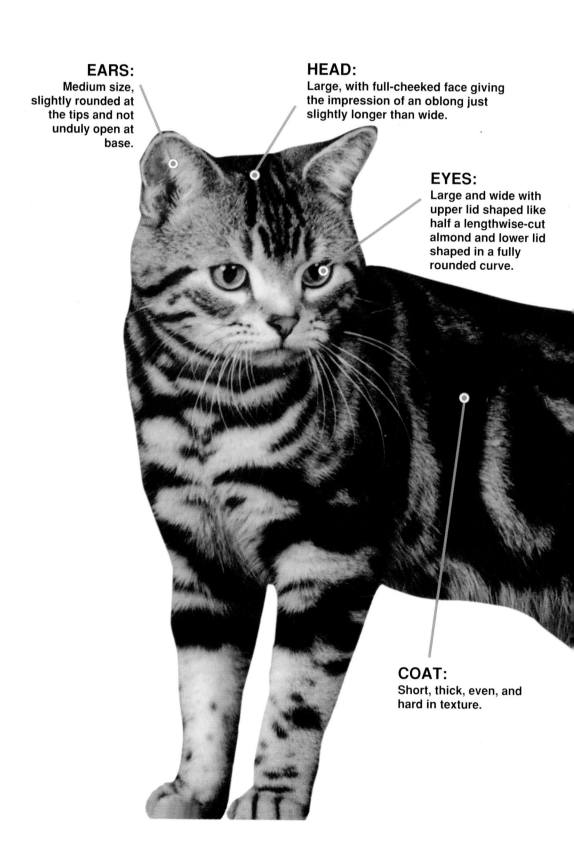

EARS:
Medium size, slightly rounded at the tips and not unduly open at base.

HEAD:
Large, with full-cheeked face giving the impression of an oblong just slightly longer than wide.

EYES:
Large and wide with upper lid shaped like half a lengthwise-cut almond and lower lid shaped in a fully rounded curve.

COAT:
Short, thick, even, and hard in texture.

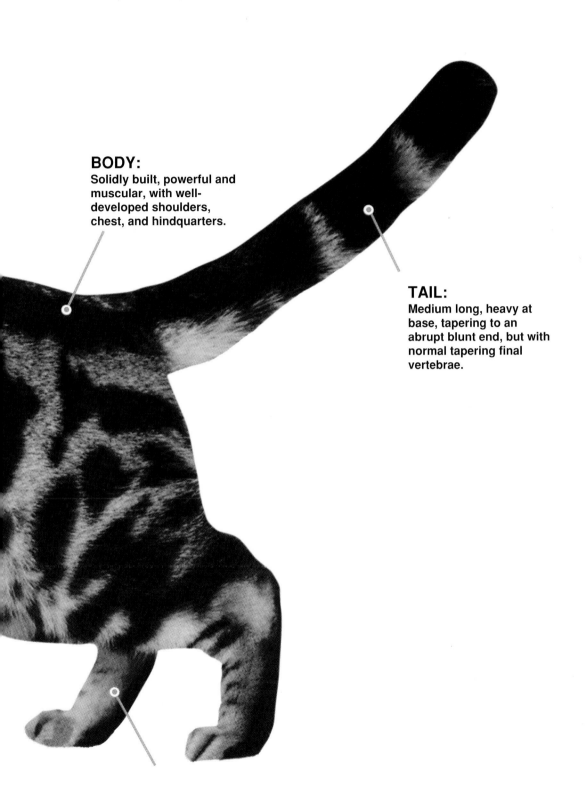

BODY:
Solidly built, powerful and muscular, with well-developed shoulders, chest, and hindquarters.

TAIL:
Medium long, heavy at base, tapering to an abrupt blunt end, but with normal tapering final vertebrae.

LEGS:
Medium in length and bone, heavily muscled.

evidence of hybridization resulting in the colors chocolate, sable, lavender, lilac, point-restricted (i.e., Siamese-type markings) or unpatterned agouti (i.e., Abyssinian-type ticked tabby). Any appearance of hybridization with any other breed, including long or fluffy fur, deep nose break, bulging eye set, brow ridge. Kinked or abnormal tail. Locket or button (white spots on colors not specifying same). Incorrect number of toes. Undershot or overshot bite. Tongue persistently protruding. Obesity or emaciation. Any feature so exaggerated as to foster weakness.

AMERICAN SHORTHAIR COLORS

The American Shorthair comes in more than 80 different colors and patterns—too many to list here individually. One of the most striking and recognizable American Shorthair cats is the silver tabby, with its dense black, classic tabby pattern on a sterling silver background.

In the cat fancy, the names used to describe some colors are not what the average person is accustomed to calling them. For example, what most cat owners commonly refer to as a gray cat is called a *blue* cat in the cat fancy. Cats that look orange are called *red.* If a cat's eyes appear to be orange, they are called copper. If that seems confusing, add to it the degrees or types of coloring— van, shell, shaded, and smoke— and the coat patterns—tabbies, calicos, and tortoiseshells—and it becomes obvious that you will find American Shorthairs in a virtual crazy-quilt of looks. Only those heavily involved in breeding, showing, and judging could ever remember them without the help of a printed list.

The color standards are quite specific and define not only what colors are acceptable but also where on the cat's body they should appear. Because of the detailed nature of the color standards, it is impossible to provide a comprehensive list here, but a sampling will give the prospective American Shorthair owner a glimpse into the world of the cat fancy as the CFA defines it.

SOLID COLORS

WHITE: Pure glistening white. **Nose leather and paw pads:** pink. **Eye color:** deep blue or brilliant gold. Odd-eyed whites will have one blue and one gold eye with equal color depth.

BLACK: Dense coal black, sound from roots to tip of fur. Free from any tinge of rust on tips or smoke undercoat. **Nose leather and paw pads:** black. **Eye color:** brilliant gold.

BLUE: Blue, lighter shade preferred, one level tone from nose to tip of tail. Sound to the roots. A sound darker shade is more acceptable than an unsound lighter shade. **Nose leather and paw pads:** blue. **Eye color:** brilliant gold.

RED: Deep, rich, clear, brilliant red, without shading, markings, or ticking. Lips and chin the same color as coat. **Nose leather and paw pads:** brick red. **Eye color:** brilliant gold.

CREAM: One level shade of buff

This handsome black feline owes her existence as an American Shorthair to both human intervention and the good graces of Mother Nature.

cream without markings. Sound to the roots. Lighter shades preferred. **Nose leather and paw pads:** pink. **Eye color:** brilliant gold.

SHADED COLORS

Cats with a shaded coat have an undercoat that is white with a mantle of tipping that shades down her sides. Acceptable American Shorthair shaded colors include silver, cameo (red), blue, and cream.

SMOKE COLORS

Smoke defines cats with a white undercoat that is tipped in the cat's basic color so that when they are in repose they appear to be the basic color. When they are in motion, the white undercoat becomes apparent. Acceptable American Shorthair smoke colors include black, blue, red, blue cream, and several color combinations.

SHELL COLORS

Shell defines a cat with a white undercoat and the coat on its back, flanks, head, and tail lightly tipped with its basic color. Face and legs may be lightly shaded with tipping. Frill, ear tufts, stomach, and chest are white. American Shorthairs come in several shell colors and color combinations.

VAN COLORS

Van is the term for a cat that is white with the additional colored portions confined to the head, tail,

If you are planning to compete in cat shows or to become a breeder, it is imperative to become familiar with the American Shorthair breed standard and to learn to recognize an outstanding specimen.

and legs as in the Turkish Van breed. One or two small portions of color on the body are allowable.

TABBY COLORS

As with the van, "tabby" describes a coat pattern, and it is this pattern in which American Shorthairs are most often seen. Tabby cats come in both the mackerel tabby pattern and the classic, or blotched, tabby pattern. The CFA recognizes both patterns in the American Shorthair.

The mackerel tabby cat has dense, clearly defined markings and all narrow pencillings. Legs are evenly barred with narrow bracelets coming up to meet the body markings. The tail is barred. Necklaces on the neck and chest are distinct, like so many chains. Head is barred with an "M" on the forehead. Unbroken lines run back from the eyes. Lines run down the head to meet the shoulders. Spine lines run together to form a narrow saddle.

The classic tabby pattern has dense, clearly defined, and broad markings that are swirled rather than striped. The legs are evenly barred with bracelets coming up to meet the body markings. Tail is evenly ringed and there are several unbroken necklaces on neck and upper chest, the more the better. Frown marks on forehead form an intricate letter "M." Unbroken line runs back from outer corner of the eye. There are swirls on the cheeks. Vertical lines over the back of the head extend to shoulder markings that are in the shape of a butterfly, with both upper and lower wings distinctly outlined and marked with dots inside the outline. Back markings consist of a vertical line down the spine from butterfly to tail with a vertical stripe paralleling it on each side, the three stripes well separated by stripes of the ground color. Large solid blotch on each side to be encircled by one or more unbroken rings. Side markings should be the same on both sides. Double vertical rows of buttons on chest and stomach.

Acceptable American Shorthair tabby colors include silver, red, brown, blue, and cream, as well as various color combinations.

CALICOS AND TORTOISESHELLS

A calico cat is white with distinct patches of black and red on her body. A dilute calico is a white cat with unbrindled patches of blue and cream. White is predominant on the underparts. Tortoiseshells have black with patches of red or softly intermingled areas of red on their bodies and extremities. Because the gene that causes the calico and tortie color pattern is a sex-linked gene, such cats are almost always female. The occasional male will be sterile.

EYE COLOR

American Shorthairs can have brilliant gold, green, or hazel eyes. The breed standard specifies for each coat color and pattern the appropriate eye colors.

These two Shorthairs enjoy a playful moment with one of their favorite toys, a feather plume.

When you buy an adult cat, no guesswork is involved in determining how the cat will turn out.

SELECTING AN AMERICAN SHORTHAIR

Now that you've decided that this sturdy breed of cat is the one for you, your next step is to make some decisions about what kind of American Shorthair you want. A little bit of planning will go a long way in helping you find a cat suitable to your personal preferences and keep you from making any costly mistakes that you may later regret. The American Shorthair has consistently been one of the top-ten most popular cats according to the Cat Fanciers' Association, so you should have no trouble finding a reputable breeder from whom to purchase your cat.

KITTEN OR CAT

The first decision you should make is how old your new cat will be. People love kittens. They are playful, inquisitive, and fun to watch. Kittens are thought to come with no bad habits and no

This American Shorthair is enjoying a quiet moment before she goes to the show ring. You should have no trouble finding a reputable dealer from whom to purchase your cat.

retraining requirements. Even so, the drawback to adopting a kitten is that she will require more constant attention and energy than an older, more mature adult cat because your home is her playground.

The adult cat, on the other hand, is one that has a developed appearance and personality. When you purchase an adult cat, what you see is what you get. No guesswork is involved in determining how the cat will turn out. If you are interested in exhibiting, the quality and conformation to the breed standard of an adult American Shorthair will be apparent. For the potential exhibitor, purchasing an adult that has competed in the ring a few times will help simplify the process of finding a show cat.

If simply finding a healthy companion animal is your primary concern, an adult will offer the same love and affection as a kitten. Breeders often sell as pets adult cats that are no longer part of the show circuit or their breeding program. Occasionally, the adult may cost less than a kitten. The disadvantages to purchasing an adult are that you will not be able to shape her character and personality or watch your cat grow up. Although the cattery environment will play an important part in her ability to adjust to her new home, an adult cat may take longer to adjust than a kitten.

MALE OR FEMALE

Generalizing about differences in the feline sexes can be as inexact as generalizing about the human ones. Just when you think you have a rule of thumb, someone comes along and points to an exception. Given an environment filled with love and affection, both male and female cats will make great pets.

If you are planning on becoming a breeder, finding a top-quality female should be your primary concern. Stud service can be provided by a male under contract from another cattery. Intact male cats engage in territorial spray marking that results in a characteristic cat odor that is offensive and difficult to eliminate, so keeping a male that is not neutered in your home can cause problems. You may not want to deal with these problems unless you are committed to becoming a breeder or can find a separate location in your home in which to maintain the cat.

The sex you choose will ultimately be a matter of personal preference. Breeders say male cats tend to be easygoing and more apt to park beside you when you sit down to read or watch television. Females are more likely to be busy doing something that interests them just when you want to cozy up with them. Your cat, no doubt, will be the exception to the rule. As a rule, male American Shorthairs are larger in size than female ones, mature males weighing from 11 to 15 pounds and mature females weighing from 8 to 12 pounds.

PET OR SHOW

The vast majority of kittens available for purchase, even from

With their cage door open, these young littermates wonder who will be checking them out.

reputable breeders, are what are commonly referred to as *pet-quality* kittens—those that do not conform to the breed standard in some way. Don't be misled into thinking that a pet-quality kitten is in some way substandard or that if you purchase one, its life will be full of health-related problems. A cat's lack of conformation will only be a problem if you intend to exhibit or breed your cat, in which case, the more closely it conforms to the standard, the better chance you have of successfully competing.

Most American Shorthair breeders keep their kittens until they are 12 to 16 weeks of age. During that time, they are able to assess the kittens and determine which ones may make the best show cats.

Breeders typically keep the best-quality kittens in a litter for part of their own breeding

programs, so purchasing a show-quality cat is more difficult than purchasing a pet-quality one. It's easier to tell if a cat is show quality if it is older and has a proven history in the show ring. If showing or breeding is your intention, ask the breeder to see the kitten's pedigree. Find out how many champions the sire and dam have produced and what titles other members of the family have won. Ask to see cats with a proven track record.

ONE CAT OR TWO

Because American Shorthairs are very social cats and like companionship, you might want to consider purchasing two instead of one, especially if no one is home during the day or if you must be away from home periodically. You will have the easiest time bringing two cats into your home if they are littermates and purchased at the same time. However, if you decide to bring a second American Shorthair into your home after purchasing the first, you can ensure successful bonding by introducing the cats gradually. Keep the new cat separate for a few days and allow both cats to smell each other from behind closed doors. Allow the new cat to have access to the rest of the house for short periods of time. Gradually increase the amount of time until both felines are acclimated to one another.

WHERE TO BUY

Although you will be able to find kittens from an array of sources—pet shops, newspaper ads, breeders, and maybe even the person in the cubicle next to you at the office—it can't be stressed too much that finding a reputable breeder from which to purchase your American Shorthair will help ensure that you find a healthy cat to be your companion for a long time. If showing or breeding American Shorthairs is in your future, it is imperative that you find a reputable breeder from whom to buy a cat that is free of contagious diseases and conforms to the standard of the breed.

Pet shops care little about where their animals come from and where they go. Because responsible breeders want to make sure their kittens are placed in good homes with people who can adequately care for them, they screen prospective buyers.

Pet shops care only that the buyer has the money to pay for the kitten. Because responsible breeders often belong to clubs that have codes of ethics prohibiting members from selling kittens to pet shops, pet shops are forced to rely on kitten and puppy mills—commercial kennels that churn out kittens and puppies simply to make a profit. Females live in cages and are kept pregnant whenever they are in heat, which can be three to four times a year. Because profit is the motive, little money is spent on veterinary care and adequate nutrition for the pregnant female or her offspring. You as the buyer will never see where the cat came from and the kind of conditions under which she was born and raised.

Pet shops also rely on the backyard breeder as supplier—the person who has a purebred female cat and wants her, for whatever reason, to have a litter of kittens. Like the mills, backyard breeders care little about the health and well-being of the offspring and where they will be placed, much less whether the kittens conform to a breed standard.

To find reputable breeders, look in the directories of the major cat magazines. Most of the national registries offer breeder referral lines that will steer you to breeders in your geographic area. Ask your veterinarian if he or she is familiar with any in your area. Look in the pet column of your local newspapers. Contact a local cat club and attend a show, not

Kittens require more constant attention and energy than mature adult cats. Your home is a kitten's playground.

only to find breeders but to see the kinds of cats they produce.

Once you have located some breeders, visit their catteries. Some registries, such as the CFA, have cattery inspection programs, which means that the catteries have been inspected by veterinarians and adhere to specific standards. The program is voluntary, and breeders must pay an inspection fee to the veterinarian and a certification fee to the CFA. The certification is good for one year from the time of inspection. You will learn a lot about the quality of the cats produced in a cattery just by visiting it and asking questions of the breeder. Do the cats appear healthy? Do they appear to conform to the breed standard? Are the cats and kittens socialized with humans or do they stay in cages? The first two to three weeks of a cat's life are the most impressionable, and early socialization plays an important role in forming the personality of a cat. It is during this time that the most important part of the socialization process takes place. Kittens left alone to amuse themselves will continue to do so as they become adults, whereas the kitten for which human contact was important will continue to seek out that contact as an adult. If the breeder is a good one, he or she will have provided the kittens with ample human contact that will help them adjust to life as companion animals.

What are the conditions under which the queen and her offspring are kept? Are pregnant females and kittens given food that meets the special nutritional requirements for their condition and age?

Expect the breeder to ask questions of you, too. Good breeders invest a lot of time, effort, and money into their cats and kittens and will want to know if you can continue to provide them with excellent care. You also will be required to sign a contract at the time of purchase that will require you to have the cat you purchase spayed or neutered, unless a legitimate breeding program is planned.

If the nearest cattery is too far away to visit, ask the breeder to send you photos of the kittens available. Most breeders will ship a kitten to you if you cannot come to get it. Regardless of the cattery's location, ask the breeder to give you references. People who have purchased kittens or cats from the breeder will be able to offer you insight into the relative quality of the cats they bought.

Early spaying and neutering is growing in acceptance. Some breeders are having their cats altered and ready to be placed at the age of 16 weeks, so you may be able to find an American Shorthair that already has had this important surgery.

A HEALTHY CAT

If the breeder is a good one, you can be sure of obtaining a healthy cat. By the time a kitten is offered for sale, she has been weaned to solid food, has received her first set of vaccinations, and has visited a veterinarian at least once. Cattery animals are routinely tested for contagious diseases. Reputable breeders offer a health guarantee that the kitten will remain healthy in a specified time period after purchase, and if she does not, the kitten will be replaced or the money refunded.

Healthy kittens and cats will be alert. Their eyes will be bright, shiny, and clear, with no watery discharge. Their ears will be clean and free of dirt. Their coats will have no bald patches or evidence of flea dirt, and the area around their tails will be clean.

GENERAL CARE AND GROOMING

Before bringing home your American Shorthair, you will need to purchase some basic items. First and foremost is a litter box. Litter boxes come in all shapes and sizes. Even if your American Shorthair is a kitten or small adult, a larger litter box will provide her with ample room to turn around and dig—a feline favorite pastime—and will prevent you from having to invest in a larger box as your cat grows. If your home or apartment is small, you might want to buy a covered box or hide it completely by purchasing one of the newer litter boxes concealed in a piece of furniture. If your local pet store does not carry the kind of box you want, check in the classified sections of the major cat magazines.

Grooming your cat will help keep loose hair to a minimum and help prevent her from getting hairballs.

You'll find just as many types of cat box filler as you will litter boxes. Clay or clumping litter or litter made from newspaper pellets, corn cobs, or wood chips—the variety is endless. Some filler requires disposal with the rest of your garbage, while other types can be flushed down the toilet. Cats seem to develop preferences for certain types of litter. Perhaps one is less dusty or softer on their feet. When you purchase your American Shorthair, find out from the breeder to what kind of litter she is accustomed, then make any changes gradually to keep litter box aversion problems from occurring.

Cats are naturally drawn to anything in which they can dig and bury their wastes, so your American Shorthair kitten will already know how to use the box when you purchase it. To help your new kitten or cat learn where the box is, show her the box immediately when you bring her home. Keeping the litter box clean is the best way to ensure that your cat continues to use it, so purchase a slotted litter scoop and remove wastes daily.

Although the American Shorthair's coat requires little maintenance, you will need to groom her regularly, including giving her a periodic bath.

In addition to digging, scratching is another favorite feline occupation. Scratching enables cats to remove the sheaths of their nails as the new nail grows in and to mark objects with their scent using glands on the pads of their feet. Some cat owners have their cats declawed, a procedure whereby the toenails, usually on the front feet, are surgically removed. You may be under contract with the breeder from whom you purchased your American Shorthair not to have it declawed. If you intend to show your cat, her claws must be intact. Cats are as naturally drawn to scratching posts as they are to their litter boxes, so providing posts made of carpet, sisal rope, or wood is an effective way to save wear and tear on your furniture and is a safe, painless alternative to declawing.

Your American Shorthair will spend up to 16 hours a day sleeping and may want to snuggle with you when you hit the sack. You might be flattered and encourage her to do so. Even if your cat has a welcome sleeping place in your bed, providing other sleeping areas around the house will help your cat feel at home and may help cat hair from accumulating on your furniture. Cats love to sleep in tight, cozy places. Fake fur kitty cups and molded beds enable your cat to curl up inside for a good night's sleep or a quick catnap. Soft foam beds that can be placed on a chair or sofa keep your cat's spirits up and cat hair deposits down. Beds can be as simple as a fabric-covered piece of foam or as elaborate as a double-decker bunk bed. You will find them in colors to match any decor.

Food and water bowls come in glass, aluminum, plastic, ceramic, and china. Plastic has an advantage in that it won't break, but plastic accumulates oils that are more difficult to remove and may exacerbate a case of feline acne—black crusty patches on a cat's chin. If you purchase ceramic or china bowls, make certain that they are lead free. Because cats don't typically drink water with their meals, avoid combination bowls that have food and water sections joined together. Place your cat's water dish away from her food bowl in another part of the kitchen or in another room altogether to encourage drinking.

Playtime will be an important part of your interaction with your American Shorthair. Provide her with safe toys to occupy her time with or without you. Interactive toys enable her to get exercise and have fun. Toys need not be expensive, either. A cat will enjoy chasing a crumpled piece of paper or sliding in a paper bag as much as playing with a more costly, complex apparatus.

A proud owner shows off her American Shorthair's general shape and coat, which is dense and waterproof due to the cat's ancient legacy as a worker in the wild.

SAFETY

Keeping your cat indoors will prevent certain accidents from happening, but your home is not totally safe unless you take steps to make it so. Many houseplants are poisonous to cats. Ingesting them can cause symptoms that range from stomach upset and vomiting to coma and death. The list of poisonous plants is extensive, so ask your veterinarian for one and eliminate any from your home or place them out of your cat's reach. To provide your cat with a fresh supply of greens to chew, plant some grass seed in a small container.

Cats like to snuggle in warm places, so keep dryer and oven doors closed. Many a cat has suffocated and died because her owner didn't know she was in the dryer when a load of clothes was put in and the machine turned on.

Keep harmful chemicals and medicines out of your cat's reach. Mothballs, cleansers, cleaning products, and human prescription or non-prescription drugs can be fatal to the cat that swallows them.

This freshly groomed cat has neatly clipped claws that won't accidentally scratch her loving owner. Clipped claws are required for cat shows.

When cleaning, remove any residue of the cleaning product to prevent your American Shorthair from getting any on her coat and then licking it off. Cats are drawn to antifreeze, so clean up any that has spilled in your garage. Antifreeze with propylene glycol instead of ethylene glycol is safer, but is still toxic if enough is ingested.

Tie up loose electrical cords if your cat seems to want to chew on them. Don't allow miniblind cords or drapery pulls to dangle and entice your kitten or cat to play and accidentally get caught in them. Keep small objects such as needles, pins, coins, and paperclips out of sight and out of mind.

One of the leading causes of accidental death, particularly for city cats, is falling from an upper-story window. Even a fall from a second-story window can be fatal, so make sure that screens are securely latched or windows are shut.

GROOMING

American Shorthairs have a coat that is short, thick, even, and hard in texture. Depending on where you live, you may find some regional and seasonal variation in coat and thickness. Because this breed has a history of life outdoors, the cat's coat is water repellent and dense enough to protect from the elements, such as moisture and cold temperatures, as well as from superficial skin injuries.

Even though the American Shorthair's short coat requires little maintenance, you will need to groom your American Shorthair regularly, including giving her a periodic bath. Because cats love to wash themselves, you may wonder why grooming is necessary. Grooming will help keep loose hair to a minimum and help prevent your cat from getting hairballs—wads of swallowed hair that form clumps that a cat expels by vomiting or that can become lodged in her digestive tract and cause blockage problems. Grooming will help you detect any fleas and discover allergic reactions that result in skin problems or bald patches.

American Shorthair breeders use a variety of grooming tools on their cats, including cotton swabs to periodically wash their ears and a damp cloth or shammy to remove excess hair and keep their coats shiny.

In the spring during the height of shedding, it's recommended that you occasionally comb your American Shorthair with a metal comb. Combining home health exams with weekly grooming sessions is a good way to keep your cat in top physical condition.

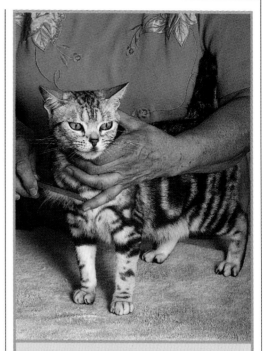

During the height of coat shedding in the spring, it is recommended that you occasionally comb your American Shorthair with a metal comb.

Your American Shorthair may keep her nails trimmed by scratching them on the post you've provided, but if you are entering a cat show, you will be required to clip the nails on all four paws. Before bathing your cat, use a nail clipper specifically made for trimming cats' nails. Hold your cat's paw and spread her toes. Look at the nails. You will notice that each has a pink area closer to the nail base. This is called the "quick." When you trim the nails, it is extremely important not to trim the quick. Trimming into the quick is extremely painful to a cat and can cause the nail to bleed.

Once your cat's nails are trimmed, move on to the bath. Cats often show an aversion to bathing, but if you are planning on exhibiting your American Shorthair, you will need to bathe and groom her prior to each show. The sooner you begin getting her accustomed to the process, the better off both of you will be. During the process, relax and make the experience a positive one for your cat. When bathing, use only a mild shampoo intended for use on cats and kittens. Make sure the room temperature is warm enough for your kitten during her bath and afterward when you towel her dry. Have clean towels handy. Fill a sink or small dishpan with warm water. If you prefer, put a bath mat on the bottom so your cat won't slide. Allow your cat to get used to standing in the water. You might want to just go this far a few times before you actually wash her. When you are applying shampoo

and working up a lather, keep it out of your cat's eyes and ears. Use a washcloth on her face and make sure you wash her hindquarters and between her toes. Thoroughly dry your cat with a blow dryer or a drying cage.

If you like, use a cream rinse or conditioner on your cat after her bath. These will keep her hair silky and help prevent dryness. Use only products intended for cats. Products intended for people and for dogs can be toxic to your cat.

A thorough teeth cleaning should be part of your cat's annual checkup, but you will need to help in between appointments. Your veterinarian will be able to supply you with a toothbrush and toothpaste intended for cats. Using it regularly and before a show will contribute to a cat's overall health and well-being.

This American Shorthair is getting a once-over—here, a judge examines her during a cat show competition.

FEEDING AMERICAN SHORTHAIRS

Up until the age of six to eight weeks, a cat's nutritional requirements are met by her mother. Once a kitten is weaned, it becomes the responsibility of her human caregiver to provide a nutritional diet to ensure growth into a healthy, happy adult and to maintain her health through the remaining stages of her life. Cats have a reputation for being finicky eaters, and what may turn on the taste buds of one feline may, in fact, turn up the nose of another. Given all of the choices of commercial and premium cat food these days, it should be relatively easy for you to find a variety of foods to keep your American Shorthair healthy and happy.

The standards by which pet food is tested and how pet food is labeled are regulated by the Association of American Feed Control Officials (AAFCO), who determine not only what goes on a label but the order in which it is presented. Reading the labels on cat food can be confusing, but it is the best way to determine whether it meets the stringent standards set up to provide your cat with optimum nutrition. Cat food that is complete and nutritionally balanced will have a guarantee on the label that reads, "Animal feeding tests using AAFCO procedures substantiate that *(brand name)* provides complete and balanced

Proper nutrition for your cat is always important. Your feline friend can reap the benefits of ultimate nutrition with healthy skin, a shiny coat, bright eyes, playful energy, and all-around good health. Photo courtesy of Nutro Products, Inc.

Should I or shouldn't I? This American Shorthair is deciding whether or not to take her vitamin supplement.

nutrition for all life stages of cats."

NUTRIENTS

Just like you, cats need certain nutrients to maintain their bodies' systems: protein, water, carbohydrates for energy, dietary fat, vitamins, and minerals. However unlike you, who could exist on a vegetarian diet that contains protein only from non-meat sources, the digestive system of a cat is built to require protein found in animal sources for optimum health. Cats are carnivores as a result of tens of thousands of years of evolution. Because of their unique metabolisms, they require from two to three times the digestible protein of their canine counterparts. Good-quality commercial food will indicate that it contains as primary ingredients protein from meat, poultry and by-products, or from seafood sources.

Protein is the source of amino acids, which are a major component of body tissue. One of the essential amino acids, taurine, has received much attention in recent years because lack of it in a cat's diet can result in feline heart and eye problems. Most commercial foods now have taurine added to the product.

Like all mammals, cats require *water* to facilitate all of their bodily processes. Cats obtain some of their water requirements from the food they eat. More water is found in canned (or wet) cat food than in dry, so a cat eating solely dry food will most likely consume more water than one eating a diet of wet food, or one that combines the wet and dry varieties.

Because today's domestic cat evolved from an ancestor that lived in the desert of Northern Africa, she is able to withstand dehydration more than you or your pet dog. Normal bodily functions such as urination, defecation, and perspiration cause your American Shorthair to lose water that must be replaced. A freshly filled water bowl somewhere

Good-quality commercial food will indicate that It contains as primary ingredients protein from meat, poultry, or seafood.

other than next to your American Shorthair's food dish will be a well-liked watering hole. Some cats prefer their water cold, so you may find your American Shorthair soliciting you to turn on the bathroom faucet or imploring you to share the jug of spring water in the refrigerator rather than partake of water that is room temperature.

Carbohydrates in the form of sugars and starches are sources of energy that help a cat metabolize other nutrients and maintain body temperature, activity level, growth, and reproduction. Although your cat can obtain adequate amounts of energy from protein and fat, most commercial pet foods contain carbohydrates.

Treats can be provided on an occasional basis to help provide a little variety in the diet. Some treats act as a cleansing agent to help reduce tartar on the cat's teeth. Photo courtesy of Heinz.

The *fat* contained in cat food provides your American Shorthair with energy and makes her food more palatable. Fat also supplies essential fatty acids that enable your cat to metabolize fat-soluble vitamins A, D, E, and K. Dietary fat will help your cat maintain a healthy, shiny coat, heal wounds, and fight infection.

Your American Shorthair needs *vitamins* for metabolism of other nutrients and for growth and maintenance. Although too little vitamin content in a cat's diet can cause health problems, too much of certain vitamins can do the same. Water-soluble vitamins, such as B-complex, niacin, and thiamin, are utilized and excess quantities eliminated. Amounts of vitamins A, D, E, and K that are not used immediately in the digestive process are stored in the body's fat. Because too much A and D can cause toxicity, veterinarians recommend that you not give your cat supplements unless you are advised to do so because of a health problem.

Your American Shorthair requires *minerals* to aid in bone growth, tooth formation, blood clotting, basic metabolism, muscle function, anemia prevention, cell oxygenation, and proper functioning of the thyroid gland. Minerals work in combination with one another, and like the other essential nutrients, are present in quantities meeting recommended allowances in good commercial and premium cat foods.

TYPES OF FOOD

Among a vast array of cat food

brands, cats and their owners may try three *types* of food as well. Although they differ in the way they are processed by pet food manufacturers, all three types can provide adequate nutrition for your American Shorthair. Read the labels carefully.

Wet—or canned—food is generally more expensive than the other types of cat food, but it is more palatable, especially if your cat is a finicky eater. Because it can contain more than 75 percent water, canned food is a good dietary source of this essential fluid. Canned food is available in sizes from 2.5 ounces to 14 ounces. Although unopened cans have a lengthy shelf life, uneaten portions must be refrigerated to maintain freshness.

Semi-moist cat food is less costly than canned but has more preservatives added to prevent spoilage of the product once the container has been opened. Many cat owners find semi-moist cat food more convenient because it can be kept for longer periods than canned food and can be free-fed to a cat without fear of it becoming contaminated as quickly as canned.

Dry is the most economical type of cat food. Because of its minimal water content, cats eat less of it than of both the wet and semi-moist varieties. Dry food may be free-fed to a cat without the fear of it attracting insects or becoming rancid when exposed to the air. Chewing dry food also provides your American Shorthair with help in keeping her teeth clean.

Regardless of the type of food you decide to feed your cat, variety is important to prevent her from relying on a food that may not be nutritionally complete. Protein

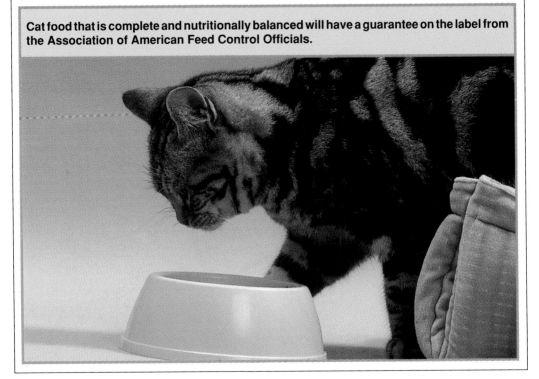

Cat food that is complete and nutritionally balanced will have a guarantee on the label from the Association of American Feed Control Officials.

should come from a mixture of meat, poultry, or fish to avoid deficiencies that might develop from consuming food from only one source—such as organ meats, red meat, or fish, for example.

HOW MUCH TO FEED

The American Shorthair has a muscular body, but size and weight may vary from cat to cat. You will want to feed a quantity that is appropriate for your cat. Many factors can affect the quantity of food your American Shorthair requires on a daily basis. These include her activity level, overall condition, age, type of food, etc. An active kitten or young cat will require a higher calorie intake than a less active adult or senior.

The bottom line is that your American Shorthair's calorie intake should match her calorie expenditure. Counting calories for

your cat can be as cumbersome and problematic as counting them for yourself, so using a basic rule of thumb will help guide you in determining correct quantities. Every cat has a layer of subcutaneous fat, but you should be able to feel her rib cage beneath the skin. A cat should not be so thin that her bones show nor so fat that you cannot feel her ribs. If you can't, your American Shorthair may be overweight and should be placed on a weight reduction program.

On food labels, manufacturers display guidelines for how much of their product to feed a cat. If you are feeding more than one type of food to your American Shorthair, it will require less of each suggested quantity than if you were feeding only one type of food.

A more recent development in pet food products is food designed for cats of different ages. You will be able to find a wide variety of foods for kittens, adult cats, and seniors. If your American Shorthair develops a health problem as she ages, such as feline lower urinary tract disease (LUTD) or kidney disease, for example, discuss the options with your veterinarian. He will be able to recommend a food product to help your cat combat her illness.

Before bringing home your American Shorthair kitten or cat, find out from the breeder or previous owner what she was fed. If you want to alter her diet, do so gradually to prevent stress or diet-related problems such as diarrhea from developing due to a sudden change in food.

Thanks to the relatively recent development of cat foods for cats of different ages, this kitten can feast on a diet created especially for her age group.

HEALTH CARE

One of your primary responsibilities as a cat owner is to provide your American Shorthair kitten or cat with good veterinary medical care. Because of their large gene pool, American Shorthairs are one of the hardiest breeds and experience no inherent health problems. They are natural cats, not bred for any extreme traits. Their muscular builds, coupled with lack of extremes in head type, contribute to their hardiness. Nevertheless, your American Shorthair will depend on you to help her stay healthy.

Preventing problems before they start is always the best medicine, and annual veterinary checkups along with good nutrition will help you keep your American Shorthair fit and healthy. By conducting a complete physical exam, your veterinarian will find most potential problems early enough to treat them. The exam includes weighing your cat;

A dental exam is an important part of this American Shorthair's annual veterinary checkup.

examining her eyes, ears, mouth, teeth, and gums; feeling for fluid buildup or bumps under the skin; and performing some simple tests, such as a fecal examination to detect internal parasites or blood tests to detect contagious diseases. You can aid in the effort throughout the year by performing home health exams and by closely observing your American Shorthair's condition and behavior to detect problems early and, if necessary, seek medical attention.

RECOGNIZING AN ILL CAT

Cats are adept at concealing illness and hiding discomfort from anyone but the most astute observer, so learning the danger signs of disease goes a long way to help protect your cat. Being able to describe a symptom will help your veterinarian diagnose the problem. Different illnesses may have similar symptoms, so the

One of the most important duties of a cat owner is providing the pet with good veterinary medical care.

more detail you can provide your veterinarian, the better chance for a positive outcome.

Illness may reveal itself in both subtle or not-so-subtle behavioral changes that may preclude overt physical signs that a health problem exists. Cats occasionally turn their noses up at the food their owners offer them, but if your cat seems disinterested in her meals altogether, it could signal a problem. If she does not eat for more than a day or exhibits other symptoms as well, contact your veterinarian. If your American Shorthair is drinking more than usual or sitting with her head hanging over the water dish, it could be a sign of dehydration due to a fever, ingestion of a toxin, or kidney problems, for example.

Changes in litter box habits, such as urinating or defecating out of the box, are often thought to be behavior problems, but they may signal that something is physically wrong, such as lower urinary tract disease or intestinal blockage. If your American Shorthair suddenly exhibits an aversion to the litter box, have

her examined by your veterinarian first before putting the cat on a behavior modification program.

If your American Shorthair turns suddenly aggressive or antisocial for no apparent reason, something physical may be the cause. Other behavioral changes that may mean your cat doesn't feel well include sleeping more than usual, hiding, crying for no apparent reason, listlessness, and loss of interest in playthings and people.

Vaccinations are in store for this healthy Shorthair that needs to be routinely protected from a number of diseases, including rabies and feline distemper.

Physical signs of illness may include vomiting or diarrhea. Cats often will vomit up a hairball or some food if it does not sit well in their digestive systems. Likewise, they may occasionally have loose bowels. However, if the vomiting is repeated, the diarrhea lasts for more than a day, or you notice blood in your American Shorthair's stools or urine, see your veterinarian.

Cats that act ill, lose their desire to wash, and exhibit a dull, lifeless coat are showing the first signs that something may be wrong. If your cat is overly licking herself or washing so much that bald patches appear on her skin, it could indicate external parasites or allergies. Other overt physical signs of illness include wheezing, gagging or retching, sneezing, tearing or watery discharge from the eyes or nose, limping, hair loss or weight loss, seizures or fits, and lumps or bumps on or under the skin.

VACCINATIONS

As part of an annual checkup, your veterinarian will vaccinate your American Shorthair against the more common feline diseases. Vaccines will force your cat's immune system to generate specialized proteins, called antibodies, that will help her develop resistance to bacteria, viruses, or toxins, and thereby fight off disease. By being exposed to particular disease antigens, your American Shorthair's immune system will fight off offending contagions if exposed. Because your cat's immunity can decrease over time, she must be revaccinated, usually annually, at the time of her veterinary checkup.

If your American Shorthair kitten has not been vaccinated already by the breeder from whom you obtained her, your veterinarian will administer a three-way series of shots called FVRCP. The shots typically are given in a series of two to three shots at three-week intervals, starting at the age of six to eight weeks.

Respiratory Diseases

FVRCP vaccines help your cat fight off feline viral rhinotracheitis (FVR) and feline calicivirus (FCV), two of the more common and contagious respiratory diseases that infect cats. Both FVR and FCV account for the majority of feline respiratory diseases. Symptoms may include sneezing, coughing, and discharge from the nose and eyes. A cat with upper respiratory disease can become dehydrated and lose her appetite. Respiratory viruses live outside the body of an animal for several hours to several days and can be transmitted from one cat to another through direct contact with infected cats; contact with contaminated cages, food and water dishes, or bedding; or even by using the litter box of a diseased cat.

Feline Distemper

The third component of the vaccine will help your cat's immune system fight feline panleukopenia (FP), or as it's more commonly called, feline distemper, a highly contagious viral disease characterized by fever, loss of appetite, dehydration, vomiting,

Cats are adept at concealing illness and hiding discomfort from anyone but the most astute observer.

and a decrease in white blood cells. Like the previous viruses, feline panleukopenia virus can be transmitted through direct contact with an infected cat; through contact with contaminated objects such as food bowls, litter pans or bedding; and by fleas. Kittens, because of their underdeveloped immune systems, are at greatest risk of contracting feline panleukopenia.

Rabies

Rabies is caused by a virus that attacks the central nervous system of warm-blooded animals, and it can be transmitted from one species of animal to another. Your American Shorthair cat can get rabies from the bite of a rabid animal or through infected saliva entering the body through an open wound, the eyes, or the mouth. Rabies is always fatal.

Keeping your American Shorthair indoors will help prevent her from contracting rabies, as well as other contagious diseases. Vaccinations will provide an extra measure of protection. Depending on where you live, you may be required by law to have your cat vaccinated against rabies and obtain booster shots every one to three years.

OTHER CONTAGIOUS DISEASES

If you obtained your American Shorthair kitten or cat from a reputable breeder, she should be free of contagious diseases at the time of purchase. Reputable breeders routinely test their cats for contagious diseases to prevent accidental spreading of disease to other cats in their catteries or to prevent breeding stock from passing diseases to their offspring.

Feline Leukemia Virus (FLV)

FLV impairs a cat's immune system and makes her more susceptible to contracting other illnesses, as well as decreasing her ability to fight off the effects of them. FLV is transmitted primarily via saliva and respiratory secretions, urine, and feces. Social grooming and licking and sharing litter boxes, food, and water bowls allow the leukemia virus to be easily transmitted from one cat to another in a multicat household. Cats roaming outdoors risk exposure via bite wounds from infected cats. A mother cat can transmit the feline leukemia virus to her offspring while they are in the uterus or while nursing.

Symptoms of FLV are often nonspecific. Poor coat appearance, loss of appetite and subsequent weight loss, lethargy, and stunted growth are some of the more common ones. Nearly one-third of cats exposed to the feline leukemia virus develop a natural immunity to the disease and never become ill. Others may become latent carriers, either never succumbing to the effects of the disease or showing symptoms under stress or during the onset of other diseases. The remaining FLV-positive cats die from the effects of the virus, usually within three years.

A test is available to detect FLV. If your American Shorthair tests positive, have her retested within three to four weeks. If the resulting tests are negative, discuss FLV vaccination options with your veterinarian.

Feline Infectious Peritonitis (FIP)

FIP is a contagious and deadly disease that, like feline leukemia, has no cure. Laboratory tests can detect the presence of antibodies to coronaviruses, of which FIP is one, but cannot specifically identify the FIP virus. Cats with the "wet" type of FIP will look extremely bloated in the abdominal area. If the fluid buildup occurs in the chest cavity, respiratory problems may occur. Other signs of FIP can include fever, loss of appetite, weight loss, and depression.

Even in catteries and multicat households, FIP is fairly uncommon. Most cats that contract FIP also have other immune-suppressing conditions such as feline leukemia. There is a vaccine available to prevent FIP, but it has aroused much controversy since its introduction. If you keep your cat indoors and away from other cats with unknown health status, you greatly lessen her chances of contracting FIP.

Feline Immunodeficiency Virus (FIV)

FIV, commonly referred to as "feline AIDS," is another immune-suppressing virus for which there is no cure. Although the virus is similar to immune-suppressing viruses in other species, including HIV, which affects humans, it cannot be passed from cat to person and vice versa.

Transmission of FIV is thought to be through bite wounds from infected cats. Symptoms of FIV are difficult to pinpoint because a host of secondary infections, such as anemia and low white blood cell count, can occur. Mouth and teeth problems such as gingivitis, stomatitis, and periodontis are often the first signs of feline immunodeficiency virus.

An antibody test will confirm the presence of the feline immunodeficiency virus, but there is no vaccine available to prevent the disease. Keeping your cat indoors and away from infected cats is the best preventive measure you can take.

PARASITES

Parasites are organisms that obtain their food by living on or in a host animal, very often at the expense of the host's health and well-being. The more common external parasites to afflict cats include fleas, mites, and ticks. Common internal parasites include tapeworms, roundworms, hookworms, and heartworm.

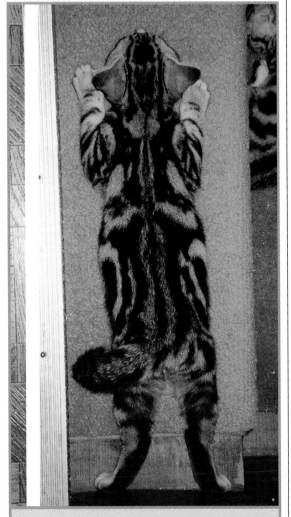

This healthy, frisky cat shows off the distinctive markings of an American Shorthair tabby.

Fleas

Among these parasites, the most common and frustrating are fleas. If they make a home with you and your American Shorthair, you may find them most difficult to expel, because not only must you eliminate the adult fleas, but also the eggs and larvae that can live up to two years in your furniture and carpet.

If your American Shorthair has become infested with fleas, you will notice flea dirt—bits of flea feces, ingested blood, and eggs—that accumulates wherever your cat may sit or sleep. Even an indoor cat can get fleas that can be carried in from the yard on your clothing and other pets. Fleas lay more eggs during warmer, more humid months, which makes them especially devastating during the summer or in warmer climates.

Fleas are not only painful and annoying to cats, but they can also produce an allergic reaction resulting in excessive licking and biting and subsequent hair loss. Keeping your American Shorthair indoors will reduce the risk of her contracting fleas, but it is no guarantee. To prevent fleas, new products in pill and liquid form have come on the market in recent years which, when given regularly, damage the flea eggs and break their life cycle.

There are a wide variety of flea products available, such as sprays, powders, dips, shampoos, soaps, and disposable dampened topical cloths, to rid your American Shorthair of fleas. Be sure to follow package directions and never mix products or use flea products intended for dogs on your cat. To eliminate fleas from the environment, foggers, misters, or premises sprays will help remove them from floors, bedding, carpet, and furniture.

Ear Mites

These appear as a brown, caked substance in a cat's ears and are microscopic parasites that can make your American Shorthair shake her head, scratch her ears, or become restless. Although ear mites are annoying to your cat, they can be treated relatively easily and eliminated with medication.

Tapeworm and Other Internal Parasites

If your cat eats infected fleas while grooming herself or decides to have an infected mouse, frog, or snake for her dinner, chances are she will develop one of three kinds of tapeworms—an internal parasite that can grow up to two feet long in your cat's body. You most likely won't notice tapeworms until tiny segments of the worm resembling rice or sesame seeds are expelled. Your veterinarian will be able to treat the tapeworm, but you must rid your cat and your house of the fleas to prevent them from recurring. Tapeworms, like all parasites, can rob your cat of her nutrition or result in a weakened immune system if they are not eliminated from your cat's body.

Other internal parasites include roundworms, hookworms, and heartworms. To detect internal parasites, your veterinarian will conduct a fecal exam as part of your cat's annual checkup. He or she will prescribe appropriate medicine to get rid of them.

SPAYING AND NEUTERING

One of the kindest things you can do for your American Shorthair and yourself is to have it spayed, if a female, or neutered, if a male. The only reason to ever let your cat remain unaltered is if she is part of a legitimate breeding program that is associated with one of the pedigreed cat registries. To breed your cat simply to generate income, to allow a female to experience producing a litter, or to allow your children to experience the miracle of birth does a disservice to you, your cat, and cats everywhere. No matter how careful a breeder you are, you cannot prevent the possibility of adding to the already overwhelming homeless cat problem. Breeding purebred cats is best left to full-time breeders.

Neutering

Neutering a tom is a relatively simple procedure. Although performed under anesthetic, neutering is usually done on an outpatient basis, and the cat is allowed to return home the same day as the surgery. Leaving your male intact will promote a host of behaviors that are unpleasant for the owner as well as anyone visiting the home. Unneutered males mark territory by spraying an anal gland secretion that produces an offensive odor that is difficult to remove or mask. Once the odor is in your home, it will perpetuate itself by arousing your male to continue to mark things around the house, not only when he detects the presence of an unspayed female but also when he detects the presence of any other cat from which he wants to protect his territory. Once a male begins to spray, this habit is more difficult to break, but neutering will help prevent this behavior from ever occurring.

Spaying

Spaying is a procedure in which the uterus of a female cat is removed. Although it is more complex than neutering, spaying is a common procedure and should not be a cause for concern. The female usually remains in the veterinary hospital for one to three days following surgery and returns about ten days later for removal of stitches.

As with male cats, unaltered females engage in behavior that causes most owners difficulty. When she enters estrus—the period of time when she is receptive to a male for the purposes of

An accidental burning on her paws from a hot surface is one of the household injuries a cat may sustain if her owner has not "cat proofed" the environment.

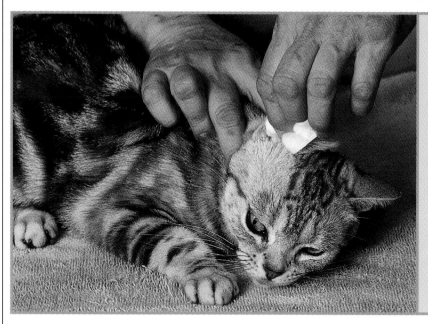

Although ear mites are annoying to your cat, they can be treated relatively easily with medication.

reproduction—an intact female will engage in behavior that is sexually suggestive to the male cat but annoying to her human companions. Rolling, crying, walking around with her posterior in the air, urinating more often, and dribbling watery discharge throughout her environment are some of the behaviors that owners of unspayed females must endure.

Veterinarians are altering cats at earlier ages, but the procedure should be performed no later than six to eight months of age. Discuss with your veterinarian the appropriate time to neuter or spay your cat.

FELINE FIRST AID

Keeping your cat indoors and cat-proofing your home will prevent a lot of accidents, but sometimes even the best efforts can result in the unexpected injury. Cats don't always land on their feet, so falling or slipping can be a problem even inside the home. Ingesting a household chemical, falling out of an upper-story window, chewing on an electrical wire, getting caught in a miniblind cord, burning paws on a hot surface, or even getting too close to a candle flame are examples of potential accidents. Being prepared might help save your cat's life in case one of these unfortunate events occurs.

If your American Shorthair sustains an accident, a knowledge of first aid will help you deal with the situation. Keep your cool. Don't wait for an emergency to hunt for appropriate phone numbers or to determine how you should deal with the situation. Acting quickly and appropriately may help save your cat's life. Keep your veterinarian's phone number and the number of an off-hours emergency clinic near your telephone in case you need them. Purchase a book on feline first aid techniques and put together a first aid kit. Keep both handy.

EXHIBITING AMERICAN SHORTHAIRS

Sooner or later as the owner of an American Shorthair, you will find yourself drawn to the world of the cat fancy, whether as an active participant exhibiting your cat in shows or as a spectator. Even if your American Shorthair is a pet-quality cat rather than a show-quality one, you are eligible to exhibit her in a cat show and compete with other pet-quality cats.

Cat shows are events where breeders, cat owners, and

It's this silver tabby Shorthair's turn to be evaluated by a cat show judge.

cat-product vendors can literally show off their wares. For the spectator, cat shows provide ample opportunities to learn about cats, new cat-related products, and what constitutes a superb specimen of the breed.

ASSOCIATIONS AND CLUBS

There are more than half a dozen pedigreed cat associations in the United States and Canada and additional ones worldwide that promote the cat fancy through regularly held shows.

Even registries based in the US can boast international members and shows held on foreign soil. Record keeping is a primary function of the registries, which maintain the pedigrees of the cats and kittens of its members and guarantee that future offspring can be registered and ancestors can be traced.

Some registries allow individual memberships, while others offer membership through regional or local cat clubs affiliated with the national association. The national and regional clubs, as well as the registries, are non-profit organizations with goals centering around the promotion of the cat

Cuddling is one way to socialize kittens that will be in for much more handling if they go on the cat show circuit.

fancy, the improvement of the individual breeds they recognize, and the welfare of cats in general. The Cat Fanciers' Association, for example, supports the Robert H. Winn Foundation, a non-profit corporation that awards grants to research feline health-related studies and sponsors an annual symposium on current feline veterinary topics. Pedigreed cat registries take an active part in the community to encourage spay/neuter awareness, and their members become active volunteers at local animal shelters.

Registries have breed councils or committees that serve as advisory bodies to the national associations. The American Shorthair breed organizations are comprised of people knowledgeable and experienced in the breed and are responsible for the continued development of the breed and for obtaining approval for modifications to the breed standard.

SHOWS

Cat shows are the heart of the cat fancy. Producing cats that conform to the standard of the breed is something to which all breeders aspire, and the cat show provides the opportunity for them not only to exhibit the fruits of their labor but also to compete with their peers for awards and prizes.

A silver tabby American Shorthair takes a brief play break during the cat show.

The first cat show, resulting in the birth of the cat fancy, took place in London's Crystal Palace in 1871. It wasn't until 1895 that a show held in New York City's Madison Square Garden marked the birth of the cat fancy in the United States.

Cat shows may be one-, two-, or several-day events, depending on the size of the sponsoring club. They can be classified as an all-breed show, in which all breeds and types of cats compete for awards, or a specialty show, in which only cats of a particular type or coat length compete.

Cat shows are held worldwide and are governed by the rules and regulations of the sanctioning registry. Even US-based associations sanction shows in foreign countries and international shows within the US. An international show is quite an event. It can attract as many as 1,000 exhibitors from all over the world and as many as 10,000 visitors a day.

JUDGING

At a show, cats are judged in separate, independently running judging rings. Cats compete against the breed standard rather than against one another. Each ring is presided over by a judge who is trained and licensed by the association in either specific breeds and categories or all breeds and categories. Depending on the registry, categories may bear the following names:

Championship: unaltered, pedigreed cats eight months of age or older;

Premiership: spayed or neutered cats eight months of age or older;

The exhibition American Shorthair must be an exemplary example of the breed and have a coat in beautiful condition.

Above: Among her older peers, this little kitten seems to be the center of attention at a cat show.

Below: Because of her coloring, this white kitten looks like a direct descendant of the first American Shorthair Grand Champion in the Cat Fanciers' Association. The winner was NorMont's Angelique, a white female born in 1948.

Kitten: pedigreed kittens aged four to eight months;

Provisional or NBC (New Breed or Color): breeds that have not yet achieved championship status;

AOV (Any Other Variety): registered cats that do not conform to breed standards;

Household Pet: mixed breed or non-pedigreed cats.

To the untrained eye, competition can seem complex and confusing. By the time a cat is entered in a show, she will already have been determined to conform to a large degree to the acceptable standard of the breed, and it will be the judge's job to determine which among many beautiful specimens comes closest.

Before entering a show, it is wise to visit several as a spectator and watch the judging. Talk to exhibitors and familiarize yourself with the breed standards and categories in which you want to enter your American Shorthair.

REGISTERING

It is common practice in the cat registries to allow an unregistered kitten to compete in a show. To be eligible to compete, adult cats must be registered. Under The International Cat Association (TICA) rules, an unregistered adult may enter a show one time before being required to register with the association. The breeder from whom you purchased your kitten will have registered the litter when the kittens were born. The registry will return certificates for the individual kittens to the breeder to be passed along to the buyer. The buyer returns the certificate with the appropriate fees to

Even if your American Shorthair is a pet-quality animal rather than a show-quality one, she is still eligible to compete with other pet-quality cats at cat shows.

the registry with the cat's chosen name to complete the process. If you have purchased an adult cat from a breeder, he or she should give you the registration at the time of purchase.

AWARDS AND PRIZES

Each registry awards predefined types of ribbons for the various categories of awards. Once a cat has collected six first-place ribbons, she becomes a Champion, after which she is eligible to compete against other Champions to garner points for Grand and Supreme Grand Champion status. Prizes awarded include ribbons, trophies, and/or cash.

Well-trained American Shorthairs pose eagerly for the camera.

Cats can register and compete in more than one registry, but points and awards do not carry over from one registry to another. A competing cat has to start at square one and compete under the rules of each different registry.

ENTERING A SHOW

Cat shows are held virtually year-round, and the dates, locations, and entry fees are advertised in the major cat publications, as well as on the World Wide Web home pages of the cat registries. Before entering, obtain a copy of the show rules, which describe entry procedures, eligibility, and exhibitor responsibility. After you have studied them, contact the entry clerk to request a show flyer and entry form. Send the completed form and fees by the deadline specified. You will receive confirmation by mail.

As you progress from local to national and international shows, the competition becomes steeper. The exhibition American Shorthair must be an exemplary example of the breed and have a coat in beautiful condition. The cat must be alert and playful, yet calm as she is being handled by the judge. Competing cats must be healthy, and in some cases, are required to have a veterinary inspection prior to the show. Your American Shorthair must be free of contagious diseases. She must be well-behaved and able to withstand the stress and rigors of the show hall environment, which include enduring a cage for most of the day, handling by judges whom she does not know, and tolerating the constant peering eyes of show spectators. Prior to the show, cats must be bathed and groomed and have their nails clipped.

Alert yet calm, this Shorthair exemplifies the kind of behavior and attitude that will serve her well in the show ring.

AT THE SHOW HALL

Once at the show, your American Shorthair will be assigned a number and a cage in what is called the benching area. Here, cats wait to be called into the judging ring. Shows typically involve a lot of commotion, but as an exhibitor you must pay attention to what is being announced over the public address system so that you don't miss being called.

Cages are typically decorated and carry the cattery name if the cats inside are being shown by a breeder. They also may display ribbons already won by their occupants. In addition to any decorations you may want, you will need a carrier for your cat, a litter box, cat beds or blankets, food and water dishes, a supply of your cat's food and water, grooming tools, a first aid kit, paper towels, vaccination certificates, and the show catalog. The show committee will provide cat litter.

If you decide to enter your cat in a show or simply attend as a spectator, make the experience an enjoyable one.

CAT REGISTRIES

How to Contact the Registries
Following are the major pedigreed cat registries in the US and Canada.

American Association of Cat Enthusiasts, Inc. (AACE)
Box 213
Pine Brook, IL 07058
913-335-6717
info@aaceinc.org
http://www.aaceinc.org

American Cat Association (ACA)
81901 Katherine Avenue
Panorama City, CA 91402
818-781-5656

American Cat Fanciers Association (ACFA)
P.O. Box 203
Point Lookout, MO 65726
417-334-5430
info@acfacat.com
http://www.acfacat.com

Cat Fanciers' Association (CFA)
Box 1005
Manasquan, NJ 08736
cfa@cfainc.org
http://www.cfainc.org/

Cat Fanciers' Federation (CFF)
Box 661
Gratis, OH 45330
937-787-9009
http://www.cffinc.org/

The International Cat Association, Inc. (TICA)
Box 2684
Harlingen, TX 78551
210-428-8046
http://www.tica.org/

Canadian Cat Association/ Association Feline Canadienne (CCA-AFC)
220 Advance Blvd., Suite 101
Brampton, Ontario, Canada
L6T 4J5
905-459-1481
office@cca-afc.com
http://www.cca-afc.com

INDEX

INDEX